Table of Contents

INTRODUCTION 1
   MY STORY 1

WHAT DOES IT MEAN TO BE GRANT READY? 5

WHAT FUNDERS WANT 7

DELIVERABLES 11
   3-RING BINDER 12
   SHARED SYSTEM IN THE CLOUD 13

TAB/FOLDER 1 - GOVERNANCE 15

TAB/FOLDER 2 - FINANCIAL 21

TAB/FOLDER 3 - LEGAL 27

TAB/FOLDER 4 - PROGRAMS 31

TAB/FOLDER 5 - PUBLIC DISCLOSURES 35

TAB/FOLDER 6 - GRANTS APPROVED 39

TAB/FOLDER 7 - FUNDER PROSPECTS 41

VIDEOCOURSE 43

NOW AVAILABLE FROM PHIL 44

MORE TESTIMONIALS 45

How To Be Grant Ready

How To Create A 3-Ring Binder & Shared System In The Cloud

By

Phil Johncock, M.A., M.Ms., GPC

Copyright © 2019 Phil Johncock

Website: www.PhilJohncock.com

NOTE: Sign up at www.PhilJohncock.com to receive discounts and coupon codes to the VideoCourse version as well as other related books and bonus material that didn't make it into this book!

All rights reserved. No part of this publication may be reproduced or transmitted in any form or by any means, electronic or mechanical, including photocopying, recording, or by any information storage and retrieval system, without permission in writing from Phil Johncock.

Introduction

WHAT IF you could get 3 times more grant funding while cutting the time it takes to write a grant proposal by 80%?

That's what happened to me. Here's my story…

My Story

In 1988, a client asked me to write a Federal proposal for $125,000 to teach English and citizenship skills to newly legalized immigrants.

It took me 100 hours to write that first grant. I took all the time I needed in order to learn what I could about grants because I didn't have any experience. I hadn't taken a class or any training prior to that.

Unfortunately, you won't write many grants if it takes you 100 hours to write the grant.

Something amazing happened to me after about 12 years of grant writing and a 92% success rate on all my grants. When I finished writing grant proposal #52, I looked down at my watch.

I noticed that it had only taken me four hours to pull everything together for that proposal.

Somehow, I had magically gone from writing my first grant proposal in 100 hours to writing my last proposal (for four times the amount of money) in only four hours.

How did I go from writing a $125,000 grant with 100 hours of work to a $420,000 grant with only 4 hours of work?

That's what this book is about!

The secret is to be GRANT READY and have a system in place before an RFP (Request For Proposal) comes from a funder, before a grant funding opportunity ever gets announced.

Whether you need $400 or $4,000 or even $400,000, this grant readiness system really works.

Which kind of a Friday would you like to have?

Imagine what it would be like if you got an RFP from a Foundation on a Monday and your proposal were due on Friday. Now, which Friday would you prefer?

1. A **Frantic Friday**... when you don't have time to spare, you're stressed out and likely stressing out those around you.
2. A **Happy Friday**... when you can take off early and enjoy your weekend.

Well, most of us would rather have a Happy Friday.

In this book, I plan to reveal how you, too, can enjoy a Happy Friday and have a system in place that organizes you for pulling together proposals faster than you ever imagined possible.

Let's get started!

Enjoy!

Phil Johncock
Grant Professional Certified (GPC)
Copyright © 2019

P.S. 20 Years Later…

A prospective client called me 20 years after I learned what I will share with you in this book. He said, "I have 10 days to complete an application for a Federal grant." He said that he, Executive Director, was planning to be out-of-town for 7 of the next 10 days.

When he asked if I could write the grant, I said, "Well, I've got 4 hours that I can give you next week, which is all you really need if you're GRANT READY. Are you GRANT READY?"

Do you think the client was grant ready?

Unfortunately, no.

Let's change that!

What Does It Mean to Be Grant Ready?

Grant Readiness is defined as the steps you take and the documents you collect prior to an RFP (Request for Proposal) being announced by a funder (i.e., foundation, corporation or government agency) that allows your agency to:

- Assess its capacity for grant seeking,
- Respond more quickly to a funding opportunity announcement,
- Get more funding in less time,
- Determine the best matches between funders and specific programs, and
- Demonstrate accountability and transparency.

  According to Charity Navigator, **"accountability** is an obligation or willingness by a charity to explain its actions to its stakeholders." "**Transparency** is an obligation or willingness by a charity to publish and make available critical data about the organization." In the public eye, accountability and transparency are at the heart of any agency's credibility. Without them, your nonprofit's credibility plummets and gaining trust back is almost impossible.

From a funding perspective, grant-ready nonprofits, schools, local government agencies and hospitals are more high performing than their counterparts who are grant-underprepared. Grant-ready organizations are more likely to get funding that those who are not. In fact, research shows that donors are willing to shift up to $15 Billion dollars annually to high performing nonprofits. (Source: *Money for Good II*)

What Funders Want

There are three basic types of U.S. grant funders:

1. Public government agencies (federal, state and local)
2. Private foundations
3. Private corporations

Much of the funding from these three funder types goes to one of over 1 million U.S. charitable nonprofits with a 501.c.3. status with the IRS.

As you begin to access your nonprofit's capacity for grant seeking, the two key questions you should be asking right now are:

1. **What specific documents do these prospective funders likely ask for?**
2. **Which of these documents can you start collecting up front?**

To answer question #1 above, let's take a look at what four (4) private grant-making foundations ask for (source: Private Foundation Directory by U.S. Senator Harry Reid) from nonprofits to which they might give money. Here are some of the documents these four private foundations ask for:

Ben and Jerry's Foundation, Inc.

**Results expected from proposed grant
**Statement of problem project will address
**Population served
**Brief history of organization and description of its mission
**Detailed description of project and amount of funding requested
**Copy of current year's organizational budget and/or project budget
**Listing of additional sources and amount of support

Caesars Foundation

**Copy of IRS Determination Letter
**Brief history of organization and description of its mission
**Copy of most recent annual report/audited financial statement/990
**Listing of board of directors, trustees, officers, and other key people and their affiliations
**Detailed description of project and amount of funding requested
**Copy of current year's organizational budget and/or project budget
**Listing of additional sources

The Cord Foundation

**Copy of IRS Determination Letter
**Brief history of organization and description of its mission
**Copy of most recent annual report/audited financial statement/990

**How project's results will be evaluated or measured
**Listing of board of directors, trustees, officers, and other key people and their affiliations
**Detailed description of project and amount of funding requested
**Copy of current year's organizational budget and/or project budget
**Listing of additional sources and amount of support

Georgia-Pacific Foundation

**Results expected from proposed grant
**Qualifications of key personnel
**Statement of problem project will address
**Population served
**Name, address, and phone number of organization
**Copy of IRS Determination Letter
**Brief history of organization and description of its mission
**How project's results will be evaluated or measured
**Explanation of why grantmaker is considered an appropriate donor for project
**Listing of board of directors, trustees, officers, and other key people and their affiliations
**Detailed description of project and amount of funding requested
**Copy of current year's organizational budget and/or project budget

What these foundations (and most others) have in common is that they are looking for similar documents that largely fall into four key categories:

- **Governance** (i.e., annual reports, list of board members, etc.)
- **Financial** (i.e., annual operating budget, IRS form 990, etc.)
- **Legal** (i.e., IRS letter of determination, etc.)
- **Program** (i.e., qualifications of personnel, problem statement, population served, budget, etc.)

The above four categories are at the core of documents you should collect up front. They constitute the first four sections of the seven (7) primary tabs/folders of your 3-ring binder and system in the cloud:

1. Governance
2. Financial
3. Legal
4. Programs
5. Public Disclosures
6. Grants Approved
7. Funder Prospects

Deliverables

According to Wikipedia, a "**deliverable** is a tangible or intangible good or service produced as a result of a project that is intended to be delivered to a customer (either internal or external)." In this case, the customer is your nonprofit agency. Deliverables are used primarily for internal purposes.

In the case of charitable nonprofits with a 501.c.3. status with the IRS, there are two deliverables that increase your capacity for grant seeking and respond more quickly to funding opportunities:

- **3-ring binder** (with tabbed sections and hard copies of docs)
- **Shared System "In The Cloud"** (with sections and digital docs)

Let's take a brief look at both and the process for creating each.

3-Ring Binder

Every nonprofit should have hard copies of important governance, financial and legal documents (i.e., annual reports, IRS Form 990, IRS Letter of Determination, list of board members, etc.). Complete lists of these documents appear in the upcoming chapters of this book along with easy-to-follow checklists. Printed copies of documents can be provided to donors upon request as well as planners who are putting together proposals for funding for your agency.

When a staff or board member needs to find an official document, she need only open the 3-ring binder and go to the appropriate tab (i.e., governance, financial, legal, etc.). Easy, right!

A 3-ring binder with important documents can be shared with Board Members as required. For example, the Chair of the Fundraising Committee can access a list of grants approved (tab 6) as well as Funder Prospects (tab 7). This binder can also be shared with the grant writer and/or grant writing team as needed. It's a great resource that saves a tremendous amount of time in planning.

Process - Here is the process to create your own 3-ring binder (with tabs):

1. Collect and print important documents (see lists in the various chapters of this book).
2. Purchase a 3-ring binder.

3. Create seven (7) tabs. Label the tabs according to the chapters (i.e., governance, financial, legal, programs, public disclosures, grants approved, funder prospects).
4. File the documents under the appropriate tab.
5. Share your Grant Ready binder with appropriate individuals, only after they have agreed to maintain confidentiality.

Shared System in the Cloud

Today, with the widespread use and availability of personal computers and the Internet, being "grant ready" also means ultimately having a system "in the cloud" for organizing and sharing electronic copies of key documents to which you need access in the near future. What used to be saved on several individuals' computers with unique filing systems can not be saved in one secure location in the cloud.

Therefore, in addition to a 3-ring binder with hard copies of key documents, another deliverable is to store digital versions of your most important documents in a secure location "in the cloud."

Two commonly used cloud-platforms used by nonprofits are Google Drive and Dropbox. I use both but prefer Google Drive. It is free and can be accessed from your Google Gmail account.

By having digital versions (i.e., .pdf, Word, .jpg, etc.) of documents, it is easier and faster for the Chair of your Fundraising Committee, Board Chair, staff, grant writer, Grant Writing Team, etc. to access documents they need when they need them. Documents can be added as necessary. Safely stored documents can be updated, revised and improved upon, with the most recent version available in the cloud. Grant writers and your Grant Writing Team can access digital versions at their fingertips.

Process - Here is the process to create your own shared system in the cloud:

1. Collect digital versions of important documents (see lists in this book).
2. Log into your Google Drive, Dropbox or secure system in the cloud.
3. Create an umbrella (parent) folder called "Grant Ready".
4. Create seven (7) (child) folders using the chapter titles in this book (i.e., governance, financial, legal, programs, public disclosures, grants approved, funder prospects).
5. Upload the documents into the appropriate folder.
6. Share the Grant Ready folder with appropriate individuals in your organization, only after they have agreed to maintain confidentiality.

Let's take a look at the documents you can start collecting to put in your tabbed sections into your 3-ring binder and into your folders in the cloud.

Let's get started with Tab/Folder 1: Governance.

Tab/Folder 1 - Governance

Tab/Folder 1 in your 3-ring binder and system in the cloud covers how your organization is governed. Recent changes in the Form 990 by the IRS for charitable nonprofits is a reflection of the increased interest in transparency and accountability in agency governance.

Here is a checklist for tab/folder 1 (Governance):

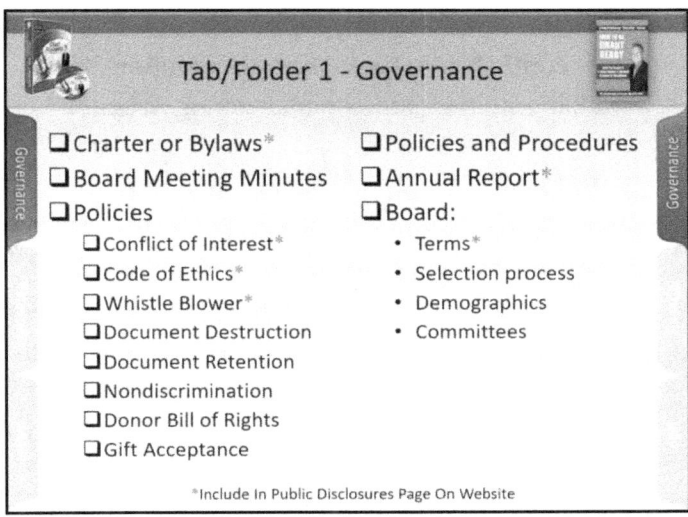

Below are the typical types of documents that U.S. charitable nonprofits might consider including in a tab on Governance.

NOTE: The asterisk next to each item means these are documents that you should include on your Public Disclosures page on your website.

- **Charter or By-laws*** – This isn't included on many nonprofit sites but it is by some.

- **Board Meeting Minutes** – Internally, approved minutes of board meetings are helpful to have for reference. Externally, it is surprising to discover just how many funders are actually asking for minutes of board and committee meetings, especially ones that document important business functions like changing the name on a checking account.

- **Policies** – A policy is an organization's official position on a certain topic. It is intended to guide decisions and actions. It addresses what should happen and why. These should be created and approved by your Board of Directors or assigned to a sub-committee to create and bring back to the Board for review and approvl.. Here are some important policies for your grant readiness 3-ring binder and cloud system:

    - *Conflict of Interest** - Your nonprofit must indicate that it has adopted a written conflict of interest policy on the IRS Form 990 (Part VI, section B, Line 12). According to the National Council of Nonprofits, it is ideal to have a process for board members to disclose conflicts of interests annually and "document in minutes of board meetings when the policy is invoked so that the nonprofit can demonstrate that compliance with the policy is regularly and consistently monitored and enforced."

❏ *Code of Ethics** - Each person on your Board of Directors should sign a Code of Ethics that speaks to appropriate behavior (i.e., respect others, participate actively, refer complaints to proper level, declare conflicts of interest, etc.) and inappropriate behavior (i.e., criticism, use of nonprofit for personal advantage, disclosing confidential information outside board room, etc.).

❏ *Whistleblower** - Your nonprofit must indicate that it has adopted a written whistleblower protection policy on the IRS Form 990 (Part VI, section B, Line 13).

❏ *Document Destruction* - Your nonprofit must indicate that it has adopted a written document destruction policy on the IRS Form 990 (Part VI, section B, Line 14).

- *Document Retention* - Your nonprofit must indicate that it has adopted a written document retention policy on the IRS Form 990 (Part VI, section B, Line 14).
- *Nondiscrimination* – Your Nondiscrimination policy might state that your agency complies to all federal statutes relating to nondiscrimination (i.e., Title VI of the Civil Rights Act of 1964 (P.L. 88-352); The Age Discrimination Act of 1975, as amended (42 U.S.C. 6101-6107), which prohibits discrimination on the basis of age; etc.
- *Donor Bill of Rights* – Your Donor Bill of Rights might include your agency's policy on fulfilling donor intent, donor restrictions and Board of Directors oversight of agency's ongoing performance in fulfilling donors' gift intent.
- *Gift Acceptance* – According to the National Council of Nonprofits, a gift acceptance policy should help "govern the receipt of 'non-cash' gifts, such as gifts-in-kind, and unusual gifts (land, vehicles, artwork, etc.)."

If you do not have these policies in place, don't panic! Just initiate the process to begin to collect, review and approve them.

If you do not have sample policies to draw from, you can download sample polices in Word, Google Docs, Pages and other formats that you can simply customize for review for your nonprofit. Visit SamplePolicies.org.

- **Processes & Procedures** – Procedures are written descriptions of the usual way of doing something. They explain how an organization wants something to be done. Not so much for funders or external stakeholders, written procedures help your internal management, staff and volunteers standardize day-to-day business operations. They lead to greater efficiency. For example, job descriptions with clear step-by-step instructions of any job -- from website design to internal accounting controls -- give clear roadmaps to any paid staff or volunteer who takes on that role.

- **Annual Report*** - It is a best practice to post your annual report on your website.

- **Board of Directors:**
    - Terms*

- ❏ Selection process (how are board members selected)
- ❏ Demographics
- ❏ Committees

*The reason there is an asterisk next to "terms" for board members should be included in your Public Disclosures page on the Internet. It comes from best practices as well as direct experience. Recently, in 2011 Assembly Bill 242 in Nevada was passed. It requires all nonprofits receiving funding from the State Department of Health and Human Resources to list board terms on their website or forfeit funding.

Originally, all agencies receiving any state funding in Nevada were to be required to post board terms on their websites. There was concern amongst legislators that nonprofits and their board were not being forthright and transparent in their operations. I include this as a "best practice" since it's pretty easy to put the information on the website and update it on a regular basis.

Tab/Folder 2 - Financial

Tab/Folder 2 includes important documents that show your accountability through your accounting and bookkeeping systems and standards.

Here is a checklist for tab/folder 2 (Financial):

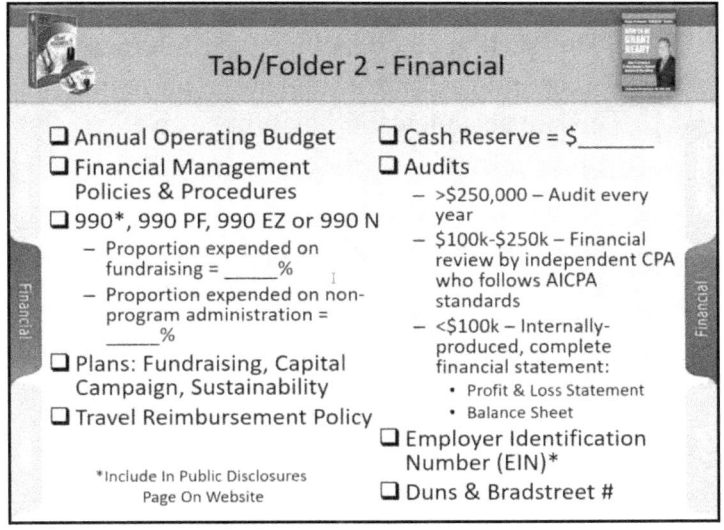

Here are some common documents to include in your Financial Tab/Folder:

❏ **Annual Operating Budget -** According to grantspace.org, "for small nonprofits with just one program, the proposal budget and organizational budget might be the same. For larger nonprofits, an organization-wide operating budget accounts for everything the nonprofit spends to carry out, evaluate and administer all its programs and activities."

❏ **Financial Management Policies & Procedures** - Is your accounting on a cash or accrual basis? Especially for small to midsize nonprofits, what are the policies and procedures, how you handle your finances? This section could include your Internal Accounting Controls that are in place to ensure accuracy and reliability as well as prevent fraud.

❏ **IRS Forms 990*, 990 PF (Private Foundation), 990 EZ (if you're under $50,000 a year) or 990 N (if you're under $50,000 as well)**. The Form 990 N is also referred to by the IRS as a postcard which is available as an electronic version.

Like the IRS Letter of Determination, the IRS also wants you to provide this information on your 990 form when anyone asks. So, you might as well put it on your website.

One of the things you may be asked by individuals and watchdog organizations like Charity Navigator is, "What proportion of your funding as expended in fundraising?" That would be a good statistic to have along with documentation that shows how you calculated that.

What Proportion is expended on non-program administration? These are things that sometimes you're going to be asked.

NOTE: These little asterisks that you'll see -- like the one next to IRS Forms 990* -- means that you should include this on your Public Disclosures page whether yours is the 990 or 990 EZ form. You won't need to include a Form 990 N but you could possibly include a screenshot if you file electronically. An asterisk means that you might consider including this document on your Public Disclosures page.

❏ **Planning Documents** – Even if you do not have strategic plans at the moment for your organization, is a "best practice" among high-performing nonprofits to have a Fundraising Plan, a Sustainability Plan as well as any strategic plan for your projects like Capital Campaigns.

I've been working a lot with clients lately on how to create Sustainability Plan upfront before they submit a proposal. With a strong Sustainability Plan in hand with well-developed strategies for implementation, their proposals stand out from the competition as being one that has buy in from the community and multiple revenue streams.

A strong Sustainability Plans shows how you're going to continue the program after grant funding runs out. Grant professionals know the major reason for getting grant funds is to get seed money to start up a project. How do you plan to sustain the program after funding runs out? And, it will!

My first grant was not a good example. I did not include was a strong Sustainability Plan. I was so excited that we got $2.5 million over five years from the federal government that I spent most of my time building the program.

It was until about Year Three of the five-year funding cycle that I began to focus on how we would be able to sustain the program.

I discovered that we would not be able to sustain it at the level that we started ($500,000 a year in funding). One of the saddest days of my life was telling over 30 teachers, over 3,000 students that they no longer had classes.

We had a national award-winning program. All the pieces were in place. Had I taken the time up front and during the program to create a Sustainability Plan upfront, things would have been different.

Moving forward, I decided that I would focus from the very start on how to sustain funding. As a result, EVERY program (now over 60) that I've been involved with has a strong Sustainability Plan up front.

What's your Sustainability Plan? Put it into your Grant Readiness binder and folders in the cloud. Include other plans as well.

❑ **Travel Reimbursement Policy** - I assume you're using the IRS standard rates for travel reimbursement. Include your policy in this tab/folder.

❑ **Audits** – One commonly-asked question I get is, "Do I need to have an audit?" Well, according to the United Way of Northern Nevada and the Sierra and its standards of excellence:

- If you're above $250,000 then you should have an audit every year.
- If you are between $100,000 and $250,000 then you should have a

> financial review by an independent CPA who follows particular standards.
> - If you're less than $100,000, then internally-produced financial statement -- Profit & Loss Statement and Balance Sheet -- will work.

69.9% of all charitable nonprofits in the U.S. have budgets less than $250,000. I imagine that many of you reading this would fall lot of you are going to fall into P&L category.

- ❏ **Employer Identification Number (EIN)***

- ❏ **DUNS Number** - The Dun & Bradstreet number is a unique nine-digit identifier for businesses. Grants.gov and the federal government (other funders as well) require you to have your Duns & Bradstreet number for your business. Getting your DUNS number is easy for you to do. It took me a minute or two to set it up for our last client. Put it in the Financial tab/folder.

*NOTE: The asterisk next to each item means these are documents that you should include on your Public Disclosures page on your website.

Tab/Folder 3 - Legal

Tab/Folder 3 includes the "legal" documents from the federal, state and local authorities regarding your agency's authority to conduct business as a charitable nonprofit.

Here is a checklist for tab/folder 3 (Legal):

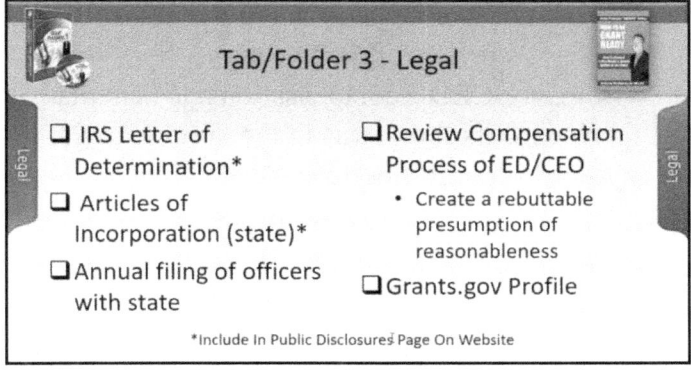

- ❏ **IRS Letter of Determination*** – This is one of the most commonly-asked-for documents that you should have readily available on your Public Disclosures page. Some states may require you to provide your IRS Letter of Determination if people ask for it. Why not have it on your website and just refer people there?

- **Articles of Incorporation** – These are a set of formal documents filed with a state government body to document the legal creation of a corporation. They usually include the nonprofit business name, street address, etc.

- **Review Compensation Process** – The National Council of Nonprofits suggests that your nonprofit agency adopt a process for the board's review of the Executive director/CEO's compensation and benefits. Nonprofits shows this in the Form 990 (Part VI, Section B, line 15).

- **Annual Filing of Officers** - Many states require you to file your list of organization officers annually. You may have this requirement in your state. If so, it may be helpful to include in your legal tab/folder proof that you have filed your list.

- **Grants.gov** – Your profile set up with Grants.gov should be kept update every year. You don't want to be in a position in which you apply for grant at the last minute. You're trying to turn in your proposal. The system won't let you. It's been more than 12 months since you've updated your profile. When you try to update your profile at the last minute, the system requires you to wait a few days for it to be updated. You miss your deadline. Keep track of updating your Grants.gov profile in your Legal tab/folder.

NOTE: The asterisk next to each item means these are documents that you should include on your Public Disclosures page on your website.

Tab/Folder 4 - Programs

Tab/Folder 4 includes details about the specific programs offered by your nonprofit. If your nonprofit organization is brand new, you may not have much in this particular tab/folder. It is helpful moving forward to add program-specific information in this section.

Here is a checklist for tab/folder 4 (Programs):

```
Tab/Folder 4 - Programs

❏ Needs Assessments &        ❏ Testimonials
   Feasibility Studies        ❏ Press Kit
❏ Mission statement*          ❏ Activity Timelines
❏ Logo*                       ❏ Forms:
❏ Organizational Chart            ❏ Accomplishments
❏ Job Descriptions                ❏ Qualifications
❏ Time Sheets                     ❏ Client population served
❏ Staff Evaluations               ❏ Performance reports
❏ Matching & In-Kind              ❏ Letters of support
   documentation                  ❏ Program budget
                                  ❏ Budget narrative
        *Include In Public Disclosures Page On Website
```

❏ **Needs Assessments** (in your community)

❏ **Feasibility Studies** (in your community)

❏ **Mission Statement***

- **Logo***

- **Organizational Chart**

- **Job Descriptions**

- **Time Sheets** - I like to have time sheets of all work performed by people hired by a grant as well as process for collecting time sheets for every project. The number one way in which nonprofits have audit problem is the inadequate documentation of the work performed. If you have time sheets for everybody who is working for your organization then you will be in really good shape.

   My timesheets are kept as an Excel document or as a Google Sheet. I have a tab for the total (month-by-month). I have tabs for each month. I include a timesheet for each program and, if required, by program category (i.e., marketing, fundraising, training, etc.). In each timesheet entry, I include:

   - Date
   - Time in
   - Time out
   - Total hours
   - Activity completed

- ❑ **Staff Evaluations** - How are you evaluating your performance? How often do you submit program reports? ... quarterly? annually? Include your reports here.

- ❑ **Matching or In-Kind Documentation** – Matching funds are those coming from other revenue sources. In-Kind are non-cash donations like volunteer time, goods and services like space rental, food, equipment, etc. Include in the Program tab/folder forms you use to document matching funding and in-kind donations.

- ❑ **Testimonials** - When you receive testimonials of your great work from your clients and stakeholders, get them in writing along with permission to use them in your promotions.

- ❑ **Press Kit** - One funder said recently that every nonprofit should go out right away and create your press kit. Include newspaper articles, videos, newsletters, flyers, publications. If you're on the radio or TV, collect these in .mp3 or .mp4 formats. It's hard to track those down after time has gone by. Having them in your Programs tab/folder when you get them will put them where you and others can go to get them when needed.

- **Activity Timelines** – I'm a strong believer that activity timelines for each program -- with action strategies, completion dates, and responsible persons -- shows all stakeholders (including funders) how you will be successful. They also show people and partners who are going to be working with you exactly what everyone is doing and "by when" things will be completed.

Additional program-specific documents that funders may ask for in their Requests for Proposals (RFPs) include:

- Agency accomplishments
- Agency qualifications
- Client/population served
- Data analysis and performance reports
- Letters of support
- Budget for program
- Budget narrative

Tab/Folder 5 - Public Disclosures

Tab/Folder 5 is a summary of items you've collected in other tabs/folders that you can display on your organization's website.

On your nonprofit's website, you can create a "parent" page called "Public Disclosures" in the navigation menu at the top or in the right sidebar. I think it is a powerful statement of accountability, transparency and even credibility to include a designated Public Disclosures webpage where everybody can find and view documents quickly.

Here is a checklist for tab/folder 5 (public disclosures):

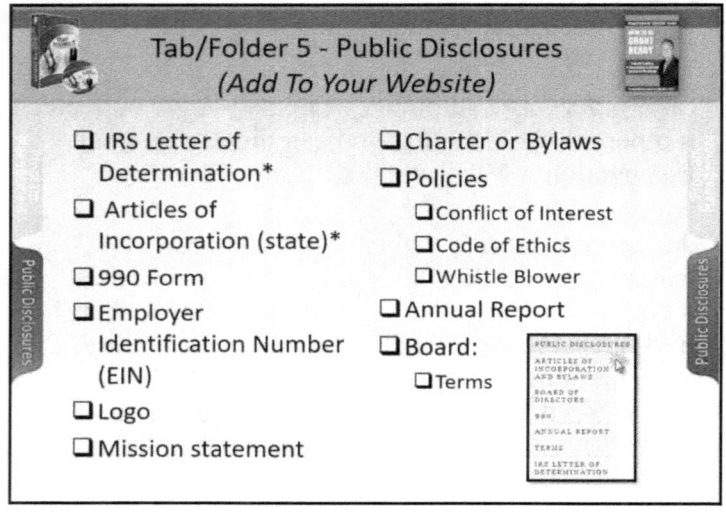

- **IRS Letter of Determination**

- **Articles of Incorporation (state)**

- **IRS 990 Form (annually)**

- **Employer Identification Number (EIN)** – Having your agency's EIN on your public disclosures page makes it easier for people to find your nonprofit on GuideStar.org and on different places online. This is particularly important if your nonprofit has gone through any name changes.

- ❏ **Logo**

- ❏ **Mission Statement**

- ❏ **Charter or Bylaws**

- ❏ **Policies**

    - ❏ Conflict of Interest
    - ❏ Code of Ethics
    - ❏ Whistleblower

- ❏ **Annual Reports**

- ❏ **Board of Directors**

    - ❏ Terms
    - ❏ List of Board of Directors (some nonprofits include headshots of their board members and/or a brief bio)

It's helpful to list your Board. List member names as well as their "terms of office."

Example: Name (term ends _____)

You can put next to their names the dates when their terms of office end. You simply <u>fill-in-the-blank</u> with the term. For example…

Sally Jones (term ends December 31, 2023)

Story: I remember sitting in the office of Senator Marilyn Fitzpatrick, state senator in Nevada. She was expressing her concern about the organizations to which the State of Nevada was giving money. She was trying to contact people on the board. She went to the website. She could not find many of the officers. Some of their terms had expired. Some of them weren't even listed.

As a result of not being able to contact people on nonprofit boards, State Senator Fitzpatrick initiated a law (AB 242) to require all agencies receiving state funds to have to put the names and term ending dates on their websites! It passed!

Tab/Folder 6 - Grants Approved

Tab/Folder 6 includes a copy of each grant application that have been approved.

Over 30 years, I have encouraged my students to create a "success log" of their grants approved. Here is one of my first personal success logs from 2002…

	Tech Prep	$	131,163.18
	Perkins III	$	347,231.84
2000-2001	School-to-Careers - Federal	$	37,000.00
	School-to-Careers - State	$	30,000.00
	Tech Prep	$	121,000.00
	Perkins III	$	425,000.00
2001-2002	School-to-Careers - Federal	$	21,634.15
	Tech Prep	$	113,263.90
	School-to-Careers - State	$	18,966.73
	Perkins III	$	400,632.50
	RTI b-ball uniforms & registration	$	1,000.00
	Softball - ASTM	$	250.00
	B-Ball - Edison Campus	$	575.00
	Regents Award - Amigo Hotline	$	7,000.00
	Regents Award - 1998-2000	$	30,000.00
Phil's Success Log 2002			**$ 5,301,191.50**
	Number of grants submitted		46
	Number of grants approved		42
	Percentage approved		91.30%

(Total Amount in Grants Received; Success Rate)

Using success logs, this is how we determined that our students received over $1.2 Billion in grant funding in 2 ½ years!

Today, I keep track of additional information using a form like this…

	Grantee/Client	Name of grant	Awarding entity	Role on the project	Dollar amount	Date/Year of award
1	Alliance for Nevada Nonprofits	Access to Housing and Economic Assistance for Development (AHEAD)	Federal Home Loan Bank of San Francisco	Manager	$25,000	Sept 2009
2	Alliance for Nevada Nonprofits	Capacity Building Grant	Citibank	Manager	$15,000	Nov 2010
3	Alliance for Nevada Nonprofits	Capacity Building Grant	Charles Schwab Bank	Writer/Manager	$10,000	Nov 2010
4	Alliance for Nevada Nonprofits	Capacity Building Grant	Wells Fargo Bank	Writer/Manager	$5,000	Jan 2011
5	Alliance for Nevada Nonprofits	AmeriCorps VISTA	Corporation for National & Community Service	Manager	$20,000	Mar 2011
6	Alliance for Nevada Nonprofits	Capacity Building Grant	US Bank	Writer/Manager	$500	Oct 2011
7	Alliance for Nevada Nonprofits	Capacity Building Grant	Charles Schwab Bank	Writer/Manager	$10,000	Nov 2011
8	Alliance for Nevada Nonprofits	Capacity Building Grant	Charles Schwab Bank	Writer/Manager	$10,000	April 2012
9	Alliance for Nevada Nonprofits	AmeriCorps VISTA	Corporation for National & Community Service	Writer/Manager	$60,810	March 2012

If you are unable to read the table above, below is a list of the items from the table of which I currently keep track regarding grant success and "grants approved":

- Grantee/client
- Name of grant
- Awarding entity
- My role on the project
- Dollar amount
- Date/year of award

Tab/Folder 7 - Funder Prospects

Tab/Folder 7 includes a list (often a spreadsheet) of prospective grant funders, deadlines, links to more information. Grant funders often include federal, state and local government agencies; private foundations with a history of giving in our geographic area; and private corporations.

In a course preparing people to pass the Grant Professional Certification (GPC) exam, I asked 20 experienced grant professionals what methods they used to track grants. Here are the most common tracking methods they reported using:

- Master calendar with submission deadlines and reporting due dates (87%)
- File folders on each potential funder with annual report, 990s, funding guidelines (74%)
- Performance report (# of grants submitted, # funded, # denied) (52%)
- A unique database they created (52%)

When you create a unique database to track your funder prospects, here are some suggested items to track on each funder:

- Geographical area of giving

- Eligibility criteria for agencies applying for funding
- Population to be served
- Deadline for applying
- Funder website
- 990-PF (private foundation)
- Annual reports
- Database used to find funder (e.g., Foundation Directory Online, GrantStation, etc.)
- Preferred method of being approached (e.g., letter of inquiry, formal proposal, website form, phone, email, office visit, etc.)
- Forms that will be required
- Type of program or agency the funder expects to fund
- Kinds of measurable outcomes expected from funded projects
- Criteria used in selecting recipients of funding
- Permitted span of time for a project (e.g., 6 months, 1 year, 3 years, etc.)
- Amount of funding the funder expects to provide
- Range of funding given in the past
- Specific support documents that should be submitted (resumes, annual budget, IRS letter of determination, mission statement, letters of endorsement, benefits formulas, indirect cost calculation, etc.)

VideoCourse Version

To access discounts and promo codes for the VideoCourse version of *How to Be GRANT READY*, visit PhilJohncock.com.

Now Available from Phil...

WIN MORE GRANTS
Like the Pros In 4 Steps
Now Available In Multi-Media Versions...

- Kindle eBook on Amazon
- Paperback on Amazon
- VideoCourse on Udemy & Simpliv
- Audiobook on Audible & iTunes

Visit PhilJohncock.com.

More Testimonials

A wealth of information.
-Tamilah Kirkendoll, Fundraiser/Development, Missouri

Vast amount of information.
-Shanelle Hurst, Minnesota

What I liked most was how complete the data was. Thank you. It really focused me.
-Katherine, Board Member, Oregon

The information was understandable and was presented at a level that was easily understood.
-Frances Williams, Louisiana

What I liked most was the very straight forward information. I was surprised by the simplicity (but crucial) organization of the binder.
-Chauntel Wright, South Dakota

What I liked most was the organization of the materials. What surprised me was documents that I have not included.
-Roxanne Powell, Pennsylvania

Concise. Concrete.
-Erik Bergh, Michigan

The binder is exactly what we are working towards to have a certified audit.
-Leslie Lynch-Wilson, Michigan

I liked it all. Clear understanding of what is needed to start process.
-Mavis Lloyd, Texas

Informative and Succinct. Very Useful.
-Amy Carrillo-Cobb, Texas

What I liked most was the organization of the binder. I was surprised by how necessary this binder is.
-Anna Buschbacher, Idaho

What I liked most was the focus on readiness and transparency.
-Will Zrnchik, California

What I liked most was the simplicity of the binder and related items per tab.
-Rene Navarro, Texas

The information was clear and concise. Being a small nonprofit, we were reassured that we are closer than we thought to completing a readiness binder.
-Brandi Ledet, Texas

Practical recommendations concerning Board and 990s. Straight-forward and simple approach.
-Edward Livingston, New Jersey

What I liked MOST was how easy it was to understand.
-Antoinette Wright, CEO/Executive Director, Illinois

What surprised me was the process developed to reduce the amount of time spent writing the proposal. What I liked most was how informative and easy to understand it was.
-Tracy Evans, Fundraiser, Nevada

Excellent explanations! What surprised me was the amount of time and thought that can be saved by using the outline and binder suggestions.
-Robin Snyder, Texas

Even though I have over 20 years of experience in grant writing, I always appreciate picking up tips about better approaches and organization.
-Nancy Azzole, North Carolina

What I liked most was the great information for helping organizations grant writing activities. What surprised me was insights provided in addition to guidance and information.
-Dale, Pennsylvania

As someone new to grant writing, this training helped me to establish a plan for organizing the documents I need. What surprised me was how much information I need to have on hand.
-Pat, Missouri

What I liked most was the information was a useful format and easy to put into practice immediately. Very informative!
-Val LaBelle, Vermont

Excellent information, especially IRS information.
-Frances Williams, Louisiana

Straightforward how-to! What surprised me most was the organization system.
-Danelle Wolf, Minnesota

What I liked most was the great visuals, clear and concise directions.
-Katrina Mari Beverly, Virginia

Great information! What surprised me is how little prepared we are.
-Kat Stratton, Georgia

What I liked most was that it is easily applicable for anyone at any experience level. What surprised me was the comprehensive information.
-Jennifer Hawthorne, Texas

What I liked most was that it gave additional information needed to prepare successful grants. What surprised me was that Public Disclosures should be on your website.
-Cassandra Crum, Georgia

What I liked most was it showed me how to maximize my time. What surprised me was how much information could be gathered in advance.
-Sharon Johnson, Louisiana

What I liked most was the 3-ring binder idea.
-George Kleeb, Nevada

What I liked most was how complete the presentation was. What surprised me was I didn't know I should have so much publicly available online.
-Abby Wheeler, Nevada

What I liked most was the very organized and useful information. What surprised me was it seems a lot more possible than I thought to be awarded a grant...if I prepare!
-Jessica Russell, Nevada

What I liked most was how simple it was.
-Naomi Leahy, Nevada

What I liked most was information about what documents are needed for grants. Also the Information about what needs to be posted on website. What surprised me was the willingness to provide the material and services to find the material needed for grants.
-Amisha Bhakta, Nevada

What I liked most was all the information given, What surprised me was the wealth of information needed on file.
-Janell Harvey, Indiana

Very informative. What surprised me was the amount of content provided.
-Jacqueline Jones, Nevada

What I liked most was the organization.
-Beverly, Virginia

What I liked most was how informative it was. What surprised me was that it was clear and easy to understand.
-Pat Pittman, Alabama

A great refresher!
-Kit DiSalvo, Wyoming

What I liked most was the specificity of the information. What surprised me was how content rich it was!
-Kathy Hix, California

What I liked most was the clarity and organization. What surprised me most was the elements that should be included on a website.
-Kathy Kennedy, Texas

What I liked the most was how informative it was! It answered a lot of my questions!
-Sharon Hughes-Foltin, Illinois

What I liked MOST was the great overview of substantial information required for preparing for grant writing.
-Paula Coggins, Texas

What I liked MOST was the time-saving and energy saving approach to write proposals. What SURPRISED ME was reducing the time spent writing the grant proposal.
-Jeffrey, Alabama

What I liked was how easy it is to set up!
- Jerry Cunningham, Arizona

What I liked MOST was the valuable info on creating a binder. What SURPRISED ME was that you could prepare 80% of info needed before you ever see an RFP.
-Treena Guy, Michigan

What I liked most was that it gave me hope. What surprised me most was how comforting it was.
-Christopher Kim, Pennsylvania

What I liked MOST was a streamlined process to gather and manage the necessary data for grant writing.
-Denise Bottomley

What I liked MOST was its conciseness.
-Dianne Sheridan, Consultant, UT

Thank you. This was very informative. Short and to the point.
-Beatrice, IL

Helped a lot and gave me great direction. What I liked MOST was the detailed information.
-Ronald, Consultant, GA

What surprised me was the depth of material. What I liked MOST was the logical organization of materials.
-Laura, Grant Writer, SC

Well-organized system. Includes a few things I hadn't thought of, and the binder system has some advantages over my system.
-Michele, Consultant, TX

This was a great way for me to begin my new experience with a nonprofit. I really think this will help me re-vitalize this organization. What surprised me was the thoroughness. What I liked MOST was the explanations.
-Stefanie, CEO/Executive Director, AZ

What surprised me was its thoroughness. What I liked MOST was the new, current, and expanded info.
-C Blanford, Grant Writer, TX

What surprised me was the clarity. What I liked MOST was the organization of information.
-CEO/Executive Director, CA

Thank you! Thank you! Thank you! What surprised me was there were documents I hadn't even thought of. What I liked MOST was giving me some structure to use in organizing all of the information I have to work with.
-Denise, Grant Writer, TX

What I liked MOST was the organization of info.
-Dianne, Grant Writer, NV

What I liked MOST was the content.
-Lillie, Staff, GA

What I liked MOST was it's practicality and ease of use.
-Matthew, Grant Writer, KS

What surprised me was it really opened my eyes to the field. What I liked MOST was the detailed list and brief explanation as to what these items are. Great tips like "Don't worry about it. You should build these policies eventually."
-Natalie, CA

What I liked MOST was everything. What surprised me was how helpful it was.
-Denise, CEO/Executive Director, NC

What I liked MOST was the content not fluff.
-Gary, Board Member, CA

What I liked MOST was the detailed information.
-Ron, Consultant, GA

A lot of good tips. What I liked MOST was getting organized.
-Lee, Grant Writer, NV

Great information. Lots of stuff I still need to learn.
-Robyn, IA

Good presentation with lots of good ideas and examples. What I liked MOST was concise details.
-Stan Hanel, Staff, NV

What surprised me was clarity and straightforwardness of something really complex. Great overview.
-Mary Ellen Saunders, Staff, IL

I'm new to this, so this helped give me direction. What surprised me was how much information was out there.
-Maria Bement, Board Member, NV

I can't wait to put our notebook together. What I liked MOST was a complete overview of the various documents to have as a part of the notebook. Readiness is the most appropriate term as putting together the notebook will lay the foundation for preparing a complete, thorough and hopefully successful grant.
-Sheryl Gonzales, Board Member, NV

What I liked MOST was showing us how to start getting organized. What surprised me was how much info is needed for public disclosure.
-Crystal Kimhan, CEO/Executive Director, NV

Wealth of information. What surprised me was the different tabs for the grant binder.
-Teresa Lewis, Grant Writer, NC

What I liked MOST was being assisted in organizing material we have on hand.
-Karen Barsell, CEO/Executive Director, NV

Very concise & helpful. What I liked MOST was how to make the binder & the contents.
-Gwen Taylor, CEO/Executive Director, NV

What I liked MOST was the detail that went into informing about the 3-ring binder. What surprised me was the simplicity of the process.
-Jeannette Wicks, Consultant, NJ

www.ingramcontent.com/pod-product-compliance
Lightning Source LLC
Chambersburg PA
CBHW070852220526
45466CB00005B/1971